MW01045789

Greek
Thought

Sophia Schreiber

Artesian **Press**

P.O. Box 355, Buena Park, CA 90621

Nonfiction
Ancient Greek Mysteries

Project Editor: Zachary N. Miller
Illustrator: Fujiko
Cover Designer: Tony Amaro
Cover Art: School of Athens, by Raphael
©2007 Artesian Press

www.artesianpress.com

 Artesian **Press**   978-1-58659-217-2

Contents

Word List

Aegean Sea (ee-JEE-ehn) A part of the Mediterranean Sea between Greece and Turkey.

Alexandria (al-ig-ZAN-dree-uh) A city in Egypt founded by Alexander the Great.

Anaximander (uh-nak-seh-MAN-der) A Greek astronomer and philosopher who argued that sunlight falling on moist ground would create life.

Anaximenes (an-ak-SIM-eh-neez) A Greek philosopher who said that everything was made up of air.

Archimedes (ar-keh-MEED-eez) A mathematician and inventor who did important work in geometry and tried to find the exact size of the number "pi." He also invented many war machines.

Aristarchus (ar-eh-STAR-kes) An astronomer and thinker who said that the world traveled around the sun.

Aristotle (ar-eh-STOT-el) Another of the most famous Greek philosophers, he wrote about science, politics and culture.

Athens (A-thenz) One of the greatest of the ancient Greek city-states, famous for its culture and democracy.

authority (uh-THOR-eh-tee) The right to give orders and be followed by others.

Babylonians (bah-beh-LOH-nee-enz) People who lived in Babylon (BAH-beh-len), an ancient civilization located in what is now southern Iraq.

biology (bie-AH-leh-jee) The study of plants and animals.

Chaos (KAY-ahs) A state of disorder and confusion. The Greeks believed that Chaos was the state of the world at the beginning of time.

civilization (siv-eh-leh-ZAY-shun) A culture that has cities, arts, sciences, and other measures of progress.

colonies (KAH-leh-neez) Cities and settlements built by a people far away from their homeland.

combination (kahm-beh-NAY-shen) A mixture or blend of two or more things, such as chemical elements.

Cynics (SIH-niks) An ancient group of thinkers who believed each person belonged to themselves, not a city or culture. In modern times, it means someone who believes people act only for selfish reasons.

democracy (dih-MAH-kreh-see) A type of government where the people vote and decide the best way to do things.

Democritus (dih-MOK-ret-ehs) A philosopher who said that the things of the world were made up of countless tiny pieces, which he called "atoms."

dictator (DIK-tay-ter) A leader who rules with total or near-total power, and often without the support of the people.

Diogenes (die-AHJ-eh-neez) A famous Cynic philosopher. He walked carrying a lantern, saying he was searching for an honest man.

Egypt (EE-jipt) An ancient nation in northeast Africa that was famous for its immense buildings. It is also a present-day nation in the same location.

element (EH-leh-ment) A basic part of something. Many Greek thinkers believed that the four main elements of the world were earth, water, air, and fire.

Empedocles (em-PED-eh-kleez) A philosopher who argued that everything in the universe was made up of four basic elements: earth, water, air, and fire.

Epicurean (ep-ih-KYOOR-ee-un) Someone who believed in Epicurus' philosophy.

Epicurus (ep-ih-KYOOR-iss) A philosopher who believed that the point of life was to gain pleasure and avoid pain.

Eratosthenes (er-eh-TAS-theh-neez) An astronomer and geographer who used geometry to figure out the size of Earth.

ether (EE-ther) An extremely light element that Aristotle believed held up the stars in the sky.

Euclid (YOO-kled) A Greek mathematician who wrote a geometry textbook that was still being used up until recent times.

government (GUH-vern-ment) An organization of people who rule and make laws for a society.

Hellen (HEL-ehn) According to Greek stories, he was the ancestor of the Greek people.

Heraclitus (her-eh-KLITE-ehs) A philosopher who said that everything is in a constant state of change. Because of this, there are no "things," and there is only change.

Hesiod (HEE-see-ed) He wrote a long poem of myths called *The Birth of the Gods*. That was his way of explaining why the world existed.

Hippocrates (hip-AK-reh-teez) A Greek doctor who was the first to realize that diseases have natural causes.

Macedonians (MAS-ih-DOH-nee-unz) People who lived in Macedon, an ancient kingdom north of Greece.

Mediterranean Sea (meh-deh-teh-RAY-nee-ehn) A large sea between Europe and Africa.

Mesopotamia (meh-seh-peh-TAY-me-eh) The region between the Tigris and Euphrates rivers in modern-day Iraq, where the first human civilizations developed.

Miletos (my-LEE-tes) A Greek city in what is now Turkey, where many of the early thinkers lived.

myth (mith) A type of story developed by ancient people. These stories gave explanations for why things were the way they were.

Noah (NOH-uh) The Hebrew prophet who was chosen by God to survive the Great Flood.

Parmenides (par-MEN-eh-deez) A Greek philosopher who said that nothing truly changes. Even though things may look like they are changing, they really are not.

Parthenon (PAR-theh-nahn) A Greek temple in Athens.

philosopher (feh-LAH-seh-fer) Something or someone who tries to find answers for the questions of life.

philosophy (feh-LAH-seh-fee) The love of knowledge and understanding.

Plato (PLATE-oh) One of the most famous Greek philosophers. He wrote *The Republic*, which discussed the concept of ideal government.

playwright (PLAY-rite) Someone who writes plays for a theater.

polis (PAH-lis) The Greek word for "city-state."

politics (PAH-leh-tiks) The science or art of government.

Prometheus (preh-MEE-thee-es) A titan (Greek giant) who stole fire from the gods and gave it to humanity.

Ptolemy (TAHL-eh-mee) He created a system of spheres that tried to explain all the movements in the sky.

Pythagoras (peh-THAG-eh-res) A philosopher who thought that everything in the world could be explained with numbers.

scientific (sie-en-TIH-fik) Having to do with, or using the rules of, science.

Sicily (SIH-seh-lee) A large island south of Italy.

Socrates (SAHK-reh-teez) Perhaps the most famous Greek philosopher, he was a teacher to Plato.

Solon (SOH-lehn) A famous ruler from ancient Athens who traveled to Egypt and asked questions.

Sparta (SPAR-teh) A city-state that was focused entirely on war.

Thales (THAY-leez) A philosopher, scientist, and thinker who believed that everything in the universe is made of water.

theory (THEE-uh-ree) An idea about the reason or cause of something.

Zeus (zoos) The king of the Greek gods.

Chapter 1

Questions

When you drop a coin on the floor, why does it bounce off a hard surface? When you throw a piece of wood into water, why does it float? If you toss a ball up in the air, why does it fall back to the ground? What is the best way for us to live?

Some of those questions are scientific (sie-en-TIH-fik). They are about the ways in which different kinds of matter behave. People we call scientists have made a lot of progress in answering these kinds of questions.

The other questions are what we might call philosophical (feh-leh-SAH-fih-kehl). They are about human nature and the way humans live with each other. Many people have come up with different answers to questions of that

15

kind. They have argued over them.

It is impossible to answer a question of either kind, of course, unless you first do something else: ask it.

Not all humans ask scientific or philosophical questions. Most people ask only questions that are about their own everyday lives. Where is the nearest store? What should I do if I cut my finger? What day is Election Day?

If you think about it, you will see that those everyday questions are really connected to the bigger questions, the scientific and philosophical ones. To get to the store, you must travel on a road, which is there only because someone once asked what kind of ground is best to walk or ride on. Good treatment of a cut is possible only because people asked many questions, over many centuries, about skin, blood, and other body parts. And there wouldn't even be an Election Day if someone hadn't wondered how to set up a government

(GUH-vern-ment).

In other words, the many good things we enjoy in our modern civilization (siv-eh-leh-ZAY-shun) exist only because some people asked questions. They exist only because some people want to know about the world.

People have been asking unusual questions for thousands of years. The Egyptians could not have built the great stone pyramids, in which they buried their dead kings, if they had not worked out the math they needed to put the stones in place. Long ago, the Babylonians (bah-beh-LOH-nee-enz) began writing down very careful records of the movements of the Sun, Moon, planets, and stars.

Around 800 B.C., long after the first people of Mesopotamia (meh-seh-peh-TAY-mee-eh) and other very ancient peoples died and became part of history, something strange happened. A new people began asking the kinds of questions that had never been asked before. These people were the Greeks.

The Greeks studied what the earlier peoples had learned about geometry, the objects in the sky, and how to bring water to their fields. If the Greeks had been like everyone else, they might simply have added a little bit to that earlier knowledge. Instead, they went further. They did not just ask, for example, "How do you make a triangle for a pyramid?" They asked, "What *is* a triangle? What kinds of rules do triangles follow?" This was very unusual.

The Greeks also began asking questions on whole new subjects. What is the nature of human beings? How should human beings behave? What is the best way for them to live with each other?

Sometimes, the Greeks got the right answers to their questions. Other times they did not. In some cases, they asked questions that were only answered hundreds of years later, by people who continued to ask questions the way the Greeks did. Some questions the ancient Greeks asked are still being asked today.

Historians often say the Greeks started Western civilization. The Greeks started the kind of thinking on which our lives are based.

The beginning of Greek thought is a great mystery. How did it start? What made the Greeks so different from other ancient peoples? Why did the Greeks start asking such good questions in the first place?

Chapter 2

The Greek World

To understand Greek thought, you first need to know a bit about where and how the Greeks lived.

Today, we think of Greeks as the people who live in the country called Greece. A map shows that it is in Europe's southeast corner.

In ancient times, the Greeks lived in that country, too. They also lived on several islands that were nearby or around it. Many Greeks lived in overseas colonies (KAH-leh-neez) that were built far away from the Greek homeland. Some of the colonies were to the north of Greece, on the coast of what we now call the Black Sea. Others were across the Aegean (ee-JEE-ehn) Sea on the coast of what we now call Turkey. Some were in the southern part of Italy

Map of the ancient Greek world

or on the island of Sicily (SIH-seh-lee), which is just off the tip of Italy. These colonies were important in world history.

The Greek homeland was not an easy land to farm. It had many mountains and few rivers. No matter where you stood in Greece, you could see a mountain. Some food came from the flocks of sheep and goats that lived on the mountainsides. The slopes were too rocky to grow crops.

The weather, too, made farming difficult. There were hot, dry summers and cool, rainy winters. In the few wide river valleys where crops could grow, farmers worked out ways to capture every drop of rain that fell on their fields.

Greece also had many earthquakes. In the valley villages, the mud-brick houses could easily be knocked down. Even with all those difficulties, the men and women still worked very hard on their small plots of land.

For many of the Greeks, the sea was more important than the land. No matter where they lived, they were not far from the Mediterranean (med-deh-teh-RAY-nee-ehn) Sea.

Solon (SOH-lehn) was a famous ruler from ancient Athens who traveled to Egypt and asked questions.

This was very helpful to the Greeks. It let them easily travel to Egypt (EE-jipt), Mesopotamia, and other places where they could learn things. During the early history of Greece, a ruler from the city of Athens (A-thenz) traveled to Egypt to ask a wise man some questions.

Ancient Greece was never just a single country. Each large city was like a country of its own. The Greek name for such a city, along with the farmland around it, was *polis* (PAH-lis). It was the word from which we got our word *politics* (PAH-leh-tiks). Polis meant "city-state" in English.

Some city-states had kings and others were ruled by a small group of landowners. Athens, the most famous city-state, was usually ruled by democracy (dih-MAH-kreh-see), which means "government by the people." Under democratic rule, every citizen of Athens was allowed to speak at the city meetings and to vote on every important issue. However, not all the people who lived in Athens were citizens. Many people were slaves.

Wars happened very often in ancient Greece, so every male citizen was also a soldier of his city. The citizens of each city trained and fought alongside their fellow citizens as equals. There were many wars between city-states. The losing city would sometimes end up being ruled by the winner. Sometimes one city-state tried to rule over many other city-states, but these little empires never lasted long. There was never a great king. There was never only one way of looking at government, or religion, or of explaining why things were the way they were.

The Greeks often argued about which form of government was the best. City-states in Greece were ruled in different ways: some were ruled by a king, some by two kings, some by a dictator (DIK-tay-ter), some by groups of important people, and some by the democratic vote of the people. If a person had ideas that were unpopular in one city-state, he or she could move to some other city where the idea was more popular or where the people weren't bothered by the idea.

Perhaps because of this, the Greeks started realizing that there were many different ways of thinking. Each city and its ideas competed with other cities and their ideas. This gave thinkers a lot of freedom. Sometimes they had to move for their own safety, but there was usually a place to go. There was no one great authority (uh-THOR-eh-tee) that made one set of ideas right and made it wrong to think about other ideas.

Did the Greeks come up with all of their interesting ideas by themselves? Or was it only because they lived next to the Mediterranean Sea and talked to other people, who sometimes had ideas of their own? Where did the Greeks get their very first ideas?

Chapter 3

Myths of Creation

Maybe the first important question that a curious person might ask is, "How did everything get here?" It is not surprising that one of the oldest pieces of Greek writing is about that very question. It is

Hesiod (HEE-see-ed) wrote a long poem called The Birth of the Gods. That was his way of explaining why the world existed.

also not surprising that the answer one Greek writer came up with was the kind of answer you would expect in most ancient writing. It was supernatural. It was about gods and goddesses.

This writing is a long poem called

The Birth of the Gods. At the beginning of time, according to the poem, there was only Chaos (KAY-ahs), or confusion. Chaos produced Darkness and Light, whose two children were Night and Day.

Chaos had another child named Earth. Earth produced Sky and Water, who then created Ocean and many other gods and goddesses. Among these was Zeus (zoos). After a big fight with his father, Zeus became king of the universe. The Greeks believed Zeus ruled over both gods and humans.

Of course, the Greeks also had to try to explain where humans came from. Their myth (mith) about that is very much like one of the stories in the Bible. It is like the story of Noah (NOH-uh) and the Flood.

In the Greek story, Zeus got angry at humans because they were wicked. He decided to wipe them out with floods. This is much like the Bible story, in which God became angry at humans.

One of the gods, Prometheus (pre-MEE-thee-es), was not happy about Zeus's plan. That was because Prometheus had a human son whom he wanted to save. He warned his son about the flood, and the son and his wife were the only humans to survive.

In the Greek story, the son of Prometheus had a son of his own, named Hellen (HEL-ehn). Hellen became the ancestor of the Greeks, which was why they called themselves Hellenes. Can you see how this story is different from the Hebrew story? Noah was saved because God favored him. With the Greeks, the humans were saved because Prometheus disobeyed Zeus.

Why do you think the first Greek thinkers believed in supernatural or religious explanations? Did they ever come up with other kinds of answers? If they did, how?

Chapter 4

Natural, Not Supernatural

If myths had been the only things that the Greeks ever thought of, there would be no reason for this book. The Greek myths are fun, but they are still only myths. They tried to explain the world the same way stories created by most other ancient peoples did. They said that all the things that happened in the world were caused by supernatural beings like gods and goddesses.

The thing that made a few Greek thinkers different from the peoples who had come before them, as well as most other Greeks, was that they didn't believe those kinds of stories. When they tried to understand the world, they stopped thinking of invisible beings. Their explanations began to be natural, not supernatural.

One of the best examples of this thinking was by a Greek doctor who was the first person to think about natural causes of sickness. He disagreed with the old-time thinkers

Hippocrates (hip-AK-reh-teez) was the first person to realize that diseases have natural causes.

who believed that illness was caused by "evil spirits." His idea of natural sickness led to modern medicine.

This new way of thinking first appeared in one of the Greek cities on the coast of what we now call Turkey. The city was named Miletus (my-LEE-tes). We could almost call it "the city where science began."

About 2,500 years ago, another thinker of Miletus started talking about his ideas. This thinker explained how he thought the world had begun. His

Thales (THAY-leez) believed that everything in the universe was made of water.

reason was not like the one in the poem. It involved no gods or goddesses. He said he thought the universe was made of water.

There was a reason that he thought this way. He pointed out that sometimes water flowed, as in a river. At other times, it was ice, which was like rock. Lastly, it was sometimes steam, which was like air. This made him think that water was the basis of everything.

Today we don't believe that theory, but that doesn't matter. What matters is that somebody was finally thinking the way a scientist does. Somebody was finally asking about the world and giving a "natural" answer.

You can see, too, that the theory

made sense. That thinker must have noticed that all the lands of the world seemed to be surrounded by water, which stretched forever. It made sense to think that everything might have come from water. He was right about some things. In modern science, we speak of matter as having three usual "states": solid, liquid, and gas. Water can be solid (ice), liquid (water), or gas (steam).

Anaximander (un-nak-seh-MAN-der) argued that sunlight falling on moist ground would create life.

Later, yet another wise man of Miletus had more natural explanations for things. He said that life was caused by sunlight that fell on moist ground. We know today that this is not true. It looked like sunlight on moist soil made life, but in truth the life was there before. It was just too small to

Anaximenes (an-ak-SIM_eh-neez) said that everything was made up of air.

see. Still, it is true that most life on earth does depend on the Sun.

Miletus produced yet another great thinker. He didn't think everything was made of water. He said everything was made of air.

According to his theory, air could turn into the different things that we see, touch, taste, and smell. When it became finer, it became fire. When it thickened, it became wind. As it got thicker, it became water and earth.

This theory was not correct. But it was another case of trying to learn why things were the way they were.

Chapter 5

Change

In the 400s B.C., Greek culture was at its most important point in history. Many of the most famous books, statues, and plays were created in that time. The people of Athens built the Parthenon (PAR-theh-nahn), a beautiful temple that often comes to our minds when we think of the ancient Greeks.

During that time, Greek thinkers wondered much about something that was a great mystery: change.

As those thinkers looked around, they saw change everywhere. A block of ice left in the sun would turn into a puddle of water, and then disappear. A tiny acorn that fell to the ground would turn into a little plant and then into a giant oak tree. The body of a dead animal would get stiff, then get mushy,

Heraclitus (her-eh-KLITE-ehs) was a philosopher who said that everything is in a constant state of change.

School of Athens:Raphael.1509

then be nothing but bones. How could these things happen? How could one "thing" be changing into another all the time?

One Greek thinker looked at the mystery of change by saying there really were no "things" at all. There was only change itself. He said that everything was changing all the time. "Everything flows."

That thinker once asked his students, "Can a man step into the same river twice?" You might think the simple answer was "Yes, of course." His answer was "No—for the river has changed, and so has the man."

Another thinker said just the opposite. He said change was not real. Even if things seem to be changing all the time, they really are not. In some way, he thought, things always stay the same. For instance, wood could be turned into paper. This seems like change,

Parmenides (par-MEN-eh-deez) said that nothing truly changes. Even though things may look like they are changing, they really are not.

but by his thinking, our senses just trick us into thinking it changed. Since the paper is made out of wood, the wood is still there.

Around the middle of the 400s B.C., a third thinker came up with an answer that was in the middle of these two ways of thinking. In the universe, he said, there really were only four things, which he called elements (EH-leh-ments). Everything was made up of combinations (kahm-beh-NAY-shens) of them. The elements were earth, water,

air, and fire.

That thinker said the four elements sometimes came together, and sometimes moved apart. He called the force that pulled them together "affection" and the force that pushed them apart "strife."

Empedocles (em-PED-eh-kleez) argued that everything in the universe was made up of four basic elements: earth, water, air, and fire.

www.presocratics.org/empedocles

Because the four elements were always coming together or moving apart, they were always ending up in different combinations. That was why there was change. The world's many different things, constantly changing from one to another, were nothing but different combinations of the elements. The elements themselves stayed the same.

We now know the usual matter of the universe is made of at least 118 basic building blocks called elements, not only four as the Greeks thought. Those elements are always being driven together or apart by forces. In their ever-changing combinations, they are rocks, trees, animals, and all the other "things" we see—including human beings.

Chapter 6

Shapes and Numbers

Democritus (dih-MOK-ret-ehs) said that the things of the world were made up of countless tiny particles called atoms.

Before the end of the 400s B.C., another Greek went even further in trying to explain change. He said all the things in the world were not made of air or water or anything else. Instead, he said, they were made of countless tiny pieces that are too small to see. He believed that everything could be divided into these pieces, but each piece itself could not be divided. He called such a piece an *atom*, which means "not divisible."

That early theory was not exactly

like our modern theory of atoms. Even so, it did include the idea that atoms were always coming together and moving apart. That was how he explained change.

Plato

School of Athens: Raphael,1509

One thinker who liked the atom idea was Plato (PLATE-oh). He lived in Athens, which was the most important city of Greece at the time. Plato opened a school to teach this new way of thinking and asking questions.

Plato liked geometry, the study of shapes. In fact, to get into Plato's school, a student first had to know about geometry.

Plato knew that other thinkers had found five shapes that they thought were perfect. He thought atoms might come in those shapes. Thousands of years later, in modern times, sci-

Pythagoras

entists found that the electron shells of atoms do have regular shapes, just as Plato thought.

Plato was not the first Greek to be interested in shapes. Back in the 500s, another Greek thinker named Pythagoras (peh-THAG-eh-res) figured out one of the most important laws, or rules, about a right triangle, which is a triangle with a square joint (a 90-degree angle).

This rule was like a magic key, which the Greeks used to unlock many secrets. They divided circles and other shapes into many right triangles. Then they used the rule to figure out other rules about all of those shapes. This was the beginning of the math that scientists have used to change our world. One modern thinker has said that the Greek who came up with this rule

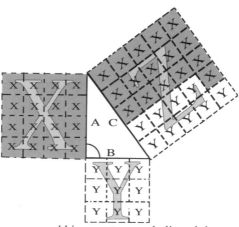

Pythagoras and his secret group believed that numbers were the key to understanding the world. His most famous secret is called the Pythagorean Theorum. He discovered that if you make a box or square from the two straight sides of a right triangle (sides A and B make squares X and Y) the area of those two squares put together (X plus Y) will always be equal to a square (Z) made from the long side of the triangle (C). Count the little boxes and see. Why is that important? Suppose you want to measure an area (the Z box) you can't get to, like a swamp, or water, or a part of outer space. You don't have to measure it. You only need to be able to measure sides A, B, and C and use Pythagoras' secret. Today people like carpenters, designers, engineers, and space scientists all use the secret every day. Now you also know it, and you didn't even need to promise to keep the secret. In this example, the numbers are even, whole numbers: 4 inches (side A), 3 inches (side B), and 5 inches (side C). Usually in real life the numbers do not come out even or whole. Ask your math teacher what Pythagoras did about that problem.

School of Athens: Raphael, 1509

Euclid (YOO-kled) wrote a geometry textbook that was still being used in recent times.

changed the world more than anyone else in history.

Pythagoras was also the leader of a group that believed the world could be understood with numbers. Pythagoras' teachings were kept secret, and members of the group would be killed if they told other people.

Alexandria (al-ig-ZAN-dree-uh) was a great Egyptian city. Though it was in Egypt, it had been built by Greeks and Macedonians (MAS-ih-DOH-nee-unz). The city had a great library that became one of the most famous places of learning in the Greek world. The thinkers who worked and studied there came up with ideas in many subjects, including geometry. One of them wrote a geometry textbook. It was still being used until recent times.

Another thinker moved from Alexandria to a Greek city in Sicily. He, too, did important work in geometry. He worked very hard to find the exact size of the strange number "pi," which is used in measuring circles.

Archimedes (ar-keh-MEED-eez) did important work in geometry, and tried to find the exact size of "pi." He also invented many war machines.

Many other ancient peoples needed to understand parts of geometry to build their cities and temples. But why did only the Greeks learn about the importance of the right triangle? Did the Greeks study only the shapes of the world? Or did they also look beyond?

Chapter 7

Earth and Sky

The Greeks' faith in shapes and numbers was a big help in another subject, the study of the solar system— Earth and its "neighborhood."

Today, schoolchildren know how the solar system works. They know day and night come because Earth turns on its axis. They know the seasons come and go because Earth tilts its north side first toward the Sun and later away from the Sun in its journey around the Sun each year. They know Earth is just one of several planets making such a trip around the Sun.

Imagine how things must have seemed in ancient times to the thinkers who were trying to figure this out. From their homes on Earth, the view of the solar system was not very good.

Each day, the sun seemed to rise in one place and set in another. It seemed like the seasons came and went for no reason. In the night sky, some objects moved in odd patterns, while others moved regularly. The Moon had a life of its own.

Those early thinkers noticed something. Night after night, one star never moved. If you faced north and raised your head high enough, you would be looking right at it. Although the other stars stayed still in relation to each other, they all went slowly around this North Star, as if it were the center of a huge wheel.

There were two ways to explain this. Either the Earth was turning beneath the stars, or the stars were turning above the Earth.

We know now that it is the Earth that is turning. Even in ancient Greece, some thinkers thought that was right, though most did not. As early as the

500s B.C., one of the thinkers of Miletus, Anaximander, who also believed sunlight caused life (see page 33), had an idea that the Earth was in the middle of a giant set of round containers shaped like wheels, with one inside the other. He thought the containers were like glass, so you could see through them. The stars were attached to the inside of one, the Sun to the inside of another, and so on. As the containers turned, people on Earth saw those objects moving in the sky.

Scientists think this was the first time somebody was trying to make sense of the universe. Anaximander's idea tried to explain the movements in the sky in a natural way. It tried to solve two other problems—things we don't even think about any more.

The first problem was to figure out what was holding the stars in place. Everyone knew that on Earth things either fell, as rocks do, or rose, as smoke does. How were the stars just staying up in the sky?

The second problem had to do with the strange objects that moved across the sky in confusing patterns. The Greeks called those objects planets, a word that means "wanderers." The Greeks knew about five of the planets.

The ancient thought had been that the planets were gods. In fact, our names for them are still the names of gods—Venus, Mercury, and so on. By explaining their movements as the turning of a container to which they were attached, Anaximander made them seem like normal objects. As for the stars, which were also thought to be gods, he said they were just rings of fire.

Plato, with his love of shapes, thought the movements of the objects in the sky must somehow be circles. Later, by about A.D. 100, another Greek thinker had the whole thing worked out. For more than 1,000 years, his

Ptolemy (TAHL-eh-mee) created a system of clear spheres, one inside the other, that tried to explain all the movements in the sky.

School of Athens: Raphael, 1509

system of clear spheres, with one inside the other, was what people thought caused movements in the sky.

Meanwhile, there was another student of Plato's. His name was Aristotle (are-eh-STOT-el). He became one of the most famous Greek thinkers of all time. He accepted the idea that everything on Earth was made of four elements. To explain why the stars did not fall, he said they were made of something else. This material, he said, was extremely light. He called it ether (EE-ther).

Other Greek thinkers added other ideas. One of them changed the whole system around so that the Sun, not the Earth, was in the middle of things. Although this was right, not many thinkers of the time agreed. Using geometry to study the shadow cast by the Earth on the Moon during a lunar eclipse, he figured out the

Aristarchus (ar-eh-STAR-kes) said that the world revolved around the Sun.

Moon's distance from Earth. Studying the angle of a shadow cast by the Sun on the first day of summer, another thinker used geometry to figure out the size of the Earth, which he was convinced was ball-shaped. Both of these measurements were almost exactly right.

Today we know that many of the Greek ideas were

Eratosthenes (er-eh-TAS-theh-neez) figured out the size of the Earth by using geometry.

wrong. There are no glass spheres. There is no ether. We know the planets, which number more than five, do not move in circles (although they do move in an oval shape, which is almost the same as a circle).

We also know how the rules of the world up in the sky are not different from the rules of the world on Earth. We know that gravity, which is what makes things fall to Earth, is the same thing that controls the movements of the planets, the Moon, and other things in outer space.

As we have seen, the Greeks asked many questions about the natural world. But did they also ask questions about human nature? What did it mean to be human?

Chapter 8

How to Live

Even while the Greeks were making their amazing advances in math and science, they began thinking about other things. As they looked around at human life, they could see that people behaved in many different ways. They began to ask, "Is there a best way to live?"

Of course, it is not unusual to wonder what is best thing to do at certain times. You might ask yourself, for example, "In this weather, should I wear my heavy coat or just my jacket?" That question is "practical," not philosophical. It is not the kind of question the Greeks asked themselves when they wondered how best to live.

One group of thinkers were called the Stoics (STO-iks). They got that

Epicurus

name because at first they met on the porch of a certain building. The Greek word for porch is *stoa*.

The Stoics thought it was important to live "according to Nature." By this they meant you should not waste energy trying to fight things you cannot change. If, for example, you were on an airplane that was going to crash, the Stoics would tell you not to get upset, not to shout or scream. Because there is nothing you can do about it, you should do the "natural" thing: stay calm. To most of us, that probably doesn't seem natural.

Another group of thinkers thought the important thing in life was to get pleasure and to avoid pain. Their leader, Epicurus (ep-ih-KYOOR-es), noticed that too much of something good can cause pain. Eating too much of a favorite food, for example, could make you sick. He warned people about that. Today, the word *Epicurean* (ep-ih-KYOOR-ee-un) means a person who is serious about things that give pleasure, such as good food.

Some Greeks thought that a person had to be independent and follow his own idea of what's good, even if other people didn't like him to do so. They were called Cynics (SIH-niks), which means "dog-like" in Greek. Cynics believed that your life belongs to you, not your city or country or culture. Cynics didn't think they had to follow the customs of society. Like dogs, they seemed to live among the Greeks but not act or think like them. Sometimes they were dirty and smelly, but they were truly free thinkers.

The most famous Cynic used to walk around with a lantern, as if he were searching for something. When

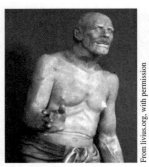

From livius.org, with permission

Diogenes (die-AH-jin-eez) was one of the Cynics. He walked with a lantern, saying he was searching for an honest man.

asked why he was doing that, he would say, "I'm looking for an honest man." The modern meaning of the word *cynic* is different from the ancient philosophy (feh-LAH-seh-fee).

Now a cynic is someone who believes people act only in their own self-interest and don't trust people who do good things.

Clearly the Greeks asked many questions about how people should act. They also came up with many answers. If they asked about how a single person should act, what did they think about how a society should act?

Chapter 9

Society

The Greeks did not think only about the way an individual person should behave. They also thought about the ways in which people lived with each other. They thought about society and government.

One of the most famous Greek writings about government is called *The Republic* and was written by Plato. *The Republic* reads like a talk among several people who argue about how to make the best society and government.

In these talks, a wise man named Socrates (SAHK-reh-teez) made the best arguments. Socrates was Plato's teacher, but by the time Plato wrote *The Republic*, Socrates was already dead. Plato simply wrote down things he remembered Socrates saying.

Socrates

en.wikipedia.org

Plato lived in Athens shortly after Athens had lost a long and terrible war against Sparta (SPAR-teh). Sparta, a city-state ruled by kings, had defeated Athens, the democracy! That made Plato think that democracy wasn't always the best form of government. In *The Republic*, Plato says it's best to be ruled by a "philosopher-king" (a truly good and wise king). Plato did have a hard time explaining how a city-state could be sure of finding such a person to become its king.

Plato's greatest student was Aristotle, who said the heavenly bodies are made of a light element called ether. After Plato's death, Aristotle set up his own school, where he studied almost everything. For example, he wrote about the shapes of many plants and animals.

This was the start of the science of biology (bie-AH-leh-jee). He also wrote about stage plays, which Greek playwrights (PLAY-rites) had invented.

Aristotle

School of Athens: Raphael, 1509

He tried to explain why people liked such plays.

Aristotle's writings about society are included in a group of essays called *Politics*. One of the very first points Aristotle made in those essays is that humans are social animals. He believed people had been made to live with each other. A person who is not able to live in society—or who does not need to—must be either a beast or a god. Aristotle meant that such a person is either less than human or more than human.

In studying things, Aristotle liked to divide them up into parts. He pointed out that a country was divided into households. In those days, the households of the rich had slaves. Aristotle thought that slavery was natural.

Aristotle studied the ways of 158 different Greek cities. He didn't think any of them was perfect. He also looked at the kind of society that had been suggested in *The Republic*. One idea in that book is that all the people in a society should own property together. Aristotle thought that was not a good idea. He thought it was difficult for humans to have too much of their lives in common, including property. He pointed out that even when people went on a trip together, they ended up fighting about many little things.

Chapter 10

Freedom to Think

All of these ideas, questions, and more came from the ancient Greeks. How can this kind of thought be explained? What was it about the Greeks that let them think about so many things in so many new ways?

By the time the Greeks arrived, human beings had been living in towns and cities for thousands of years. People first made stone tools and then bronze ones. They too had been making stone buildings, painting pictures, and carving statues for a long time. All of these things certainly required thought. The Greeks learned many things from the people who came before them. The Greeks added many ideas and asked questions that people had never thought of before.

The thinking of the Greeks was different. The Greeks did not ask, "How should we build this stone temple to the sun god?" They asked, "Is the sun really a god? If not, then what is it?" The Greeks were the first people who really thought about why the world worked they way it did.

Other societies in ancient times were usually parts of empires or large kingdoms. Choices were made by just a few people: the rulers and their families or friends. Members of this ruling class did not want anyone to ask, "What is the best kind of society?" They already thought they knew what the best kind was. It was the kind in which they were in charge. In Greece, there was no empire. Instead, each city-state governed itself as best it could in its own way, and competed with other city-states. Because the population was small, each person was important.

Religion was also different in Greece.

Priests were important, but not as powerful as they were in other lands. Each city-state had its own priests and beliefs, usually centered around a special god that watched over that city.

The Greeks had government officials, but members of the upper class did not usually have special rights. In Sparta, men called themselves "the equals."

A few Greeks did ask the most interesting questions and by so doing changed the world. Of course, no one really knows why only the Greeks asked those questions. Maybe it was because of the small city-states and their different kinds of thought. Or maybe it just happened for no particular reason.

Once, a Greek gave a definition of happiness. He said happiness was the excellent use of one's abilities. That is a truly Greek thing to think.

Bibliography

Couprie, Dirk L. "Anaximander." Internet Encyclopedia of Philosophy. 2006. http://www.utm.edu/research/iep/a/anaximan.htm

Cromer, Alan. Uncommon Sense – The Heretical Nature of Science. New York: Oxford University Press, 1993.

Fowler, Michael. "Galileo and Einstein." 1995-6. http://galileoandeinstein.physics.virginia.edu/

Hammond, Lewis M. "Epicurus." World Book Encyclopedia. Chicago, IL: Field Enterprises Educational Corporation, 1962.

Stow, H. Lloyd. "Deucalion." World Book Encyclopedia. Chicago, IL: Field Enterprises Educational Corporation, 1962.